D1140694

BOOZY
SLUSHIES, POPTAILS
& ICE POPS

BOOZY
SLUSHIES, POPTAILS
& ICE POPS

DELICIOUS RECIPES
FOR ALCOHOL-INFUSED
FROZEN TREATS

HANNAH MILES
PHOTOGRAPHY BY
ALEX LUCK

RYLAND PETERS & SMALL
LONDON • NEW YORK

For Diana, a true friend and cocktail expert

Senior Designer Sonya Nathoo
Commissioning Editor
Alice Sambrook
Production Mai-Ling Collyer
Editorial Director Julia Charles
Art Director Leslie Harrington
Publisher Cindy Richards

Food Stylist Lorna Brash
Prop Stylist Luis Peral
Indexer Vanessa Bird

First published in 2018 by
Ryland Peters & Small
20–21 Jockey's Fields
London WC1R 4BW and
341 E 116th Street, New York, 10029
www.rylandpeters.com

10 9 8 7 6 5 4 3 2 1

ISBN: 978-1-84975-966-3

A CIP record for this book is
available from the British Library.
US Library of Congress CIP data
has been applied for.

Printed in China

CONTENTS

INTRODUCTION

It's summer, the sun is shining and the day is heating up –
why should kids be the only ones having fun with frozen treats?
The recipes in this book revamp the popular icy treats from
childhood by lacing them with your favourite boozy tipples.
Stored in the freezer, they are perfect for whipping out at
a moment's notice. Follow my hints and tips below for perfect
boozy slushies, poptails and ice pops every time!

FREEZING ALCOHOL

Low-proof alcohols freeze more
easily than high-proof. I'm sure
you have had the experience of
forgetting about a bottle of wine
or beer in the freezer and coming
back the next day to find it solid!
Hence also, you can keep a bottle of
vodka in the freezer at home ready
to drink chilled without it freezing.
Therefore, it is very important to
stick to the quantities of alcohol
outlined in these recipes. The ice
pops especially, as they may not
freeze if you add extra alcohol. Also,
take note of the alcohol content
percentage on your own bottle,
if it is a particularly strong variety,
it might be worth reducing the
amount you add.

MOULDS

The ice pop moulds available to
purchase online come in a wide
range of materials, shapes and
sizes, from hard plastic to silicone
and from rectangles, to stars,
push-pops and rockets. The recipes
in this book are based on a variety
of differently-shaped moulds which
each hold about 100 ml/generous
$1/3$ cup liquid. If your moulds hold
a different volume, then adjust the
quantities in the recipe accordingly.
If you don't have any moulds to
hand, you can improvise with small
silicone cake moulds or paper cups.
It's important to note that when
liquids freeze they expand slightly,
so be careful not to completely fill
your moulds right to the top.

FIXING STICKS

Fixing the ice pop sticks properly upright is important so that your ice pops can be easily removed and don't end up wonky. Some moulds have lids with holes where you can insert your sticks, or even built-in sticks. You can create a make-shift mechanism by clipping the sticks between new, clean clothes pegs and balancing the pegs on top of the mould so that the stick is positioned in the middle. You could also cut holes in the centre of small squares of cardboard, then balance them over the top of the moulds.

UNMOULDING AND FRAGILITY

Ice pops made with alcohol can be fragile, so you need to take care when removing them from their moulds. Either remove from the freezer and leave at room temperature for a few minutes first, or run the bottom and sides of the moulds very quickly under hot water for a few seconds before carefully removing. Take care not to run under water for too long or get water on the ice pops themselves.

STORAGE

Once you have removed your pops from the moulds, you can return them to the freezer stored in sealed ziplock/plastic bags. The pops are best eaten within three months.

CRUSHING ICE

There are several methods for crushing ice to make slushies. You want finely crushed crystals that are still large enough that they do not immediately melt when they come into contact with liquids. Many blenders have an ice setting which shows they have a suitable motor for crushing ice, not all blenders do. Some fridges have a function which creates crushed ice in a few seconds. If you are really into your frozen treats, it is worth investing in a snow cone machine – these are relatively inexpensive and create perfect ice shavings for a slushie or snow cone. Or, you can place ice cubes in a doubled-up layer of ziplock/plastic bags and crush them with a rolling pin – it does not make the best ice crystals but it can be quite therapeutic!

POPTAILS

NECTARINE AND PEACH BELLINI POPTAILS

A peach bellini is a classic Italian Prosecco cocktail made with peach purée. Here, I've flavoured the delicate bubbles with peach schnapps and added a fresh fruity nectarine ice pop to turn it into a perfect poptail. It makes a really refreshing and indulgent summer treat, which looks elegant served with slices of fresh peach in the glass.

FOR THE ICE POPS
2 ripe nectarines
70 ml/2¼ oz. peach schnapps

FOR THE BELLINIS
400 ml/14 oz. chilled Prosecco
2 tablespoons peach schnapps
slices of ripe peach or nectarine, to garnish

blender, 2 thin ice pop moulds and sticks, 2 Champagne flutes

SERVES 2

Prepare the ice pops first, as they need time to freeze. Remove the stones/pits and any wooden stems from the nectarines. Place them in the blender with the peach schnapps and blitz to a very smooth purée. (I like to leave the skins on so that I have small pink flecks in the ice pop, but you can peel away the skins if you prefer.) Pour the purée into the ice pop moulds and insert the sticks in a straight, upright position. Freeze for at least 8 hours or overnight until solid.

To serve, divide the Prosecco between the two flutes and add a tablespoon of the peach schnapps to each. Remove the ice pops from their moulds (see page 7) and place in the glasses. Add peach or nectarine slices to garnish and serve straight away.

COCO-UNICORN POPTAILS

The unicorn trend is one I embrace, what's not to love about glitter and rainbows? I use thin moulds so that these coconut pops resemble unicorn horns when placed in the cocktails.

FOR THE ICE POPS
200 ml/6³/₄ oz. whole milk
80 ml/2³/₄ oz. coconut cream
1 tablespoon sugar

FOR THE COCKTAILS
250 ml/8¹/₂ oz. coconut water

10 ice cubes
100 ml/3¹/₂ oz. coconut rum
125 ml/4 oz. coconut milk
2 tablespoons grenadine
2 tablespoons blue curaçao

TO DECORATE
rainbow sprinkles
1 egg white

2 ice pop moulds, and sticks, 2 glasses, cocktail shaker, bar spoon

SERVES 2

Prepare the ice pops first, as they need time to freeze. Whisk together the milk, coconut cream and sugar until the sugar has dissolved. Pour the mixture into the ice pop moulds and insert the sticks in a straight, upright position. Freeze for at least 8 hours or overnight until solid.

For the decoration, pour the rainbow sprinkles onto a plate. Whisk the egg white and place onto another plate. Dip the glass rims into the egg white first and then straight away in the sprinkles. Set aside.

For the cocktails, add the coconut water, ice, rum and coconut milk to the cocktail shaker and shake vigorously until chilled. Pour into the two prepared glasses through a strainer to remove the ice. Use a bar spoon to pour a tablespoon of grenadine into each glass, followed by a tablespoon each of blue curaçao. They will settle at the bottom in two distinct layers.

Remove the ice pops from their moulds (see page 7) and immediately place one ice pop in each glass. Serve straight away.

WATERMELON AND TEQUILA POPTAILS

This poptail is based on a frozen margarita with its sweet, salty and sour flavours, delicious with these watermelon pops.

FOR THE ICE POPS
250 ml/8¹/₂ oz.
   watermelon
40 ml/1¹/₄ oz. tequila
squeezed juice of 2 limes
100 ml/3¹/₂ oz. clear
   sparkling lemonade
pinch of salt

FOR THE MARGARITAS
squeezed juice of 4 limes
120 ml/4 oz. tequila
120 ml/4 oz. triple sec
pinch of salt
30 ice cubes
2 tablespoons sugar
   syrup

TO DECORATE
1 egg white
flaked sea salt
watermelon slices and
lime wedges

*4 ice pop moulds and
sticks, blender, 4
margarita glasses*

SERVES 4

Prepare the ice pops first, as they need time to freeze. Remove any seeds from the watermelon flesh and place in the blender with the tequila, lime juice, lemonade and salt. Pour the mixture into the ice pop moulds and insert the sticks in a straight, upright position. Freeze for at least 8 hours or overnight until solid.

To prepare the glasses, whisk the egg white and place onto a plate. Place the salt flakes onto another plate. Dip the rim of each glass into the egg white followed by the salt, so that you have a rim of salt around the edge of each glass. Set aside.

For the frozen margaritas, add all the ingredients to the blender and blitz until the ice is crushed and the drink is blended.

Divide the frozen margarita mixture between the prepared glasses, pouring in carefully so that you do not lose the salt rims. Remove the pops from their moulds (see page 7) and place in the glasses. Add melon slices and lime wedges to garnish and serve straight away.

BLOOD ORANGE
BUCKS FIZZ POPTAILS

A bucks fizz cocktail was the height of sophistication back in the day, and it remains a firm favourite of mine. In my family we drink it on Christmas morning when opening presents. This recipe adds the traditional orange juice component in ice pop form. Here I've used blood orange in the ice pop, which gives a lovely vibrant colour. Feel free to mix and match with other fruit juices such as grapefruit, lemon or lime – all are delicious!

FOR THE ICE POPS

200 ml/6³/₄ oz. blood orange juice

200 ml/6³/₄ oz. clear sparkling lemonade

15 ml/¹/₂ oz. grenadine

TO SERVE

4 small glasses of chilled Champagne or Prosecco

blood orange slices

4 thin ice pop moulds (that will fit into Champagne flutes) and 4 sticks, 4 Champagne flutes

SERVES 4

Prepare the ice pops first, as they need time to freeze. Whisk together the blood orange juice, lemonade and grenadine in a jug/pitcher. Pour into the moulds and add the lolly sticks in a straight, upright position. Freeze for at least 8 hours or overnight until solid.

To serve, half-fill the Champagne flutes with Champagne or Prosecco. Remove the blood orange ice pops from their moulds (see page 7) and place in the glasses. Garnish with blood orange slices and serve straight away.

KIWI MARTINI POPTAILS

These vibrant green poptails, with a tangy refreshing sharpness from the kiwi, make a fun and stylish drink to serve to friends after dinner. When frozen, the kiwi seeds add a little crunch and the fruit takes on a sherbet tang. Kiwi syrup (such as the Monin brand) is available from online retailers and is worth investing in for these delicious poptails.

FOR THE ICE POPS

4 ripe kiwi fruits, peeled

100 ml/3$\frac{1}{2}$ oz. clear sparkling lemonade

1 tablespoon kiwi syrup

FOR THE MARTINIS

240 ml/8 oz. gin

80 ml/2$\frac{3}{4}$ oz. vermouth

4 tablespoons kiwi syrup

12–15 ice cubes

blender, 4 straight-sided silicone ice pop moulds and 4 sticks, cocktail shaker, 4 martini glasses

SERVES 4

Prepare the ice pops first, as they need time to freeze. Cut one kiwi into four thick 1 cm/$\frac{1}{3}$ inch slices and set aside. Place the remaining three kiwis into the blender and blitz to a smooth purée. Add the lemonade and kiwi syrup and blitz again. Pour the mixture into the silicon moulds. Press a stick through the middle of a slice of kiwi and position the slice on top of the mixture with the stick upright. Repeat for the other sticks and moulds. Freeze for at least 8 hours or overnight until solid.

For the martinis, place the gin, vermouth and kiwi syrup into the cocktail shaker with the ice and shake hard until chilled. Pour the martini through a strainer and divide into the glasses. Remove the ice pops from their moulds (see page 7) and place in the glasses. Serve straight away.

POMEGRANATE FIZZ POPTAILS

These rosé wine ice pops are made extra pretty by the addition of pomegranate seeds, although you could use strawberries or raspberries if you prefer. Served in glasses of the remaining sparkling pink wine, they make delightful summer tipples.

200 ml/6¾ oz. sparkling rosé wine
200 ml/6¾ oz. clear sparkling lemonade
1 teaspoon rose syrup
4 tablespoons pomegranate seeds

TO SERVE
chilled sparkling rosé wine
food-safe rose petals

4 ice pop moulds and 4 sticks, 4 glasses

SERVES 4

Mix together the rosé wine, lemonade and rose syrup in a jug/pitcher. Place a spoonful of pomegranate seeds into each of the ice pop moulds and pour over the rosé wine mixture. Some of the seeds will float and some will stay at the bottom of the ice pop. Add the sticks in a straight, upright position. Freeze for at least 8 hours or overnight until solid.

To serve, pour some sparkling rosé wine into each glass. Remove the ice pops from their moulds (see page 7) and place in the glasses. Garnish with rose petals, if liked, and serve straight away.

ROCK LOBSTER POPTAILS

With flavours of rum, banana and coconut, the rock lobster is a sunshine cocktail – the kind that should be savoured on the beach as the sun sets on a tropical paradise. The bright red grenadine is a homage to the drinks namesake – the lobster. If you can't find banana liqueur, then simply blitz the coconut milk with a ripe banana instead and freeze in the same way.

FOR THE BANANA LAYER
75 ml/2½ oz. banana liqueur
290 ml/10 oz. coconut milk
125 ml/4 oz. clear sparkling lemonade

FOR THE RED LOBSTER LAYER
40 ml/1¼ oz. clear sparkling lemonade
30 ml/1 oz. grenadine

TO SERVE
160 ml/5½ oz. coconut rum
160 ml/5½ oz. dark rum
dash of grenadine
maraschino cocktail cherries

4 ice pop moulds and sticks, 4 glasses

SERVES 4

Prepare the banana layer of the ice pops first. Whisk together the banana liqueur, coconut milk and lemonade in a jug/pitcher. Divide between the moulds, filling only about four fifths of the way full to leave space for the red lobster layer. Add the sticks in a straight, upright position. Freeze for at least 8 hours or overnight until solid.

For the red lobster layer, whisk together the lemonade and grenadine. Pour into the moulds on top of the banana layer, filling almost to the top. Freeze again for at least 8 hours or overnight until solid.

To serve, divide both rums between the glasses (about 40 ml/1½ oz. each). Add a dash of grenadine to each, which will sink to the bottom. Remove the ice pops from their moulds (see page 7) and place in the glasses. Garnish the drinks with a maraschino cherry and/or other kitsch decorations and serve straight away.

AMENDOA AMARGA POPTAILS

Amendoa amarga is a delicious bitter almond liqueur from Portugal. While in Vilamoura in Portugal, I drank it served over ice with fresh lemon juice to counter the sweetness of the liqueur. This poptail is one of my favourites in the book, with cherry and almond ice pops to dip into your lemon almond liqueur, the flavours complement each other perfectly. You can use amaretto if you can't get hold of amendoa amarga, or any other shaped mould if you haven't got a sphere-shaped one.

FOR THE ICE POPS
75 ml/2½ oz. amendoa amarga or amaretto almond liqueur
160 ml/5½ oz. cherry juice

TO SERVE
120 ml/4 oz. (4 x 30 ml/ 1 oz. shots) amendoa amarga or amaretto almond liqueur
squeezed juice of 2 lemons

4 sphere ice pop moulds (or other moulds) and 4 sticks, 4 small cocktail glasses

SERVES 4

Mix together the almond liqueur and cherry juice in a jug/pitcher. Pour into the sphere (or other) moulds and add the sticks in a straight, upright position. Freeze for at least 8 hours or overnight until solid.

To serve, pour a shot of the almond liqueur into each glass, then add the squeezed juice of half a lemon to each. Remove the cherry ice pops from their moulds (see page 7) and place in the glasses. Serve straight away.

CAIPIRINHA POPTAILS

Brazil's national drink is the caipirinha. Created with crushed fresh limes mixed with brown sugar and cachaça (a spirit made with fermented sugar cane), it's deliciously tangy and sour tasting. In a modern twist, this poptail has a sour lime ice pop added to the glass to sup with the cocktail.

FOR THE ICE POPS
squeezed juice of 2 limes
200 ml/6³/₄ oz. water
50 g/¹/₄ cup white sugar
3 drops of green food
  colouring (optional)

FOR THE CAIPIRINHA
SLUSHIES
2 limes, cut into wedges,
  plus extra to garnish
  (optional)
4 teaspoons light brown
  soft sugar
120 ml/4 oz. cachaça
20–30 ice cubes, crushed

*2 Ice pop moulds and
2 sticks, muddler stick (or
wooden spoon), strong
serving glasses*

SERVES 2

Prepare the ice pops first, as they need time to freeze. Mix the lime juice with the water and sugar in a jug/pitcher until the sugar has dissolved. Add a little food colouring to make the pops go bright green. (Note: omit this if you wish, but when lime juice freezes it can go brown, so I prefer mine with a little added colour.) Pour into the moulds and add the sticks in a straight, upright position. Freeze for at least 8 hours or overnight until solid.

For the slushies, divide the lime wedges and sugar between the glasses and crush together with the muddler stick (or end of a wooden spoon) to release the lime juice and make a paste with the sugar. Divide the cachaça between the glasses and stir. Add half the crushed ice to each glass and stir again to make a slushie consistency. Remove the pops from their moulds (see page 7) and place in the glasses. Garnish with extra lime wedges and serve.

ICE POPS

PIMM'S ICE POPS

Served over ice with fresh fruit, a glass of Pimm's No. 1 Cup and lemonade is the perfect summer drink. On warm, sunny days, why not make these cooling adults-only ice pops which are laced with Pimm's? They look so pretty packed with fresh mint, strawberries and nectarines.

100 ml/3¹/₃ oz. Pimm's
  No. 1 Cup
300 ml/10 oz. clear
  sparkling lemonade
10 small fresh
  strawberries, leaves
  removed, hulled and
  sliced
1 ripe nectarine, stoned/
  pitted and thinly
  sliced
12 fresh mint leaves

*4 ice pop moulds and
4 sticks*

MAKES 4

Mix the Pimm's and lemonade together in a jug/pitcher. Divide the sliced strawberries and nectarines and the mint leaves evenly between the ice pop moulds but take care not to over-fill as you want there to be enough room for the Pimm's. You might have some fruit left over.

Pour the Pimm's mixture into the ice pop moulds and add the sticks in a straight, upright position. Freeze for at least 8 hours or overnight until solid.

When ready to serve, remove the Pimm's pops from their moulds (see page 7) and serve straight away.

COSMOPOLITAN ICE POPS

The cosmopolitan is a classy, classic cocktail, and famously Carrie Bradshaw's drink of choice in Sex and the City. It has dangerously drinkable fresh and fruity flavours, with a lovely citrus tang that comes from lime juice and triple sec. I have used lime slices to garnish these pops but you could add orange slices instead for a different colour combo and fruity flavour.

300 ml/10 oz. cranberry
   juice
1 tablespoon white sugar
20 ml/³/₄ oz. triple sec
10 ml/¹/₃ oz. vodka
3 fresh limes

4 ice pop moulds and
4 sticks

MAKES 4

Mix together the cranberry juice and sugar in a jug/pitcher until the sugar has dissolved. Add the triple sec, vodka and juice of 2 of the limes and mix together. Slice the third lime into thin slices and place one into each of the ice pop moulds.

Pour the cranberry juice mixture into the ice pop moulds and add the sticks in a straight, upright position. Freeze for at least 8 hours or overnight until solid.

When ready to serve, remove the cosmopolitan pops from their moulds (see page 7) and serve straight away.

CHILLI CHOCOLATE AND BRANDY POPS

Chocolate, chilli/chile and brandy make a perfectly topsy-turvy warming combination in a frozen ice pop! This recipe is inspired by evenings spent with my Grandma Goodwin in Mallorca, drinking delicious hot chocolate laced with brandy.

FOR THE DARK/
BITTERSWEET
CHOCOLATE LAYER
100 g/3½ oz. dark/
    bittersweet chilli/chile
    flavoured chocolate,
    chopped
250 ml/8½ oz. whole
    milk

FOR THE WHITE CHOCOLATE
LAYER
125 ml/4 oz. whole milk
60 g/2 oz. white
    chocolate, chopped
20 ml/¾ oz. brandy

*4 ice pop moulds and
4 sticks*

MAKES 4

Prepare the dark/bittersweet chocolate layer first. Put the chilli/chile chocolate into a small saucepan with the milk. Simmer over a gentle heat, stirring all the time, until the chocolate has melted. Leave to cool, then stir again and pour into the moulds, filling them up two-thirds of the way full. Add the sticks in a straight, upright position. Freeze for at least 8 hours or overnight until solid.

While the first layer is freezing, make the white chocolate layer. Put the milk, white chocolate and brandy in a saucepan. Simmer over a gentle heat, stirring all the time, until the chocolate has melted. Leave to cool, then refrigerate until needed. Give the white chocolate mixture a stir and pour into the moulds on top of the frozen dark chocolate layer. Leave to freeze again for 8 hours or overnight until solid.

When ready to serve, remove the ice pops from their moulds (see page 7) and serve straight away.

GIN AND TONIC ICE POPS

The gin and tonic has become a very popular choice of drink, but one of those where personal preference is key – not only are there now a multitude of flavoured gins, but you can also add lemon or cucumber to serve to taste. These pops are very light and refreshing, you can even serve them in a glass of gin and tonic if you wish, to turn them into fun poptails!

4 thin slices of cucumber
4 thin slices of lemon,
    preserved in lemon
    juice
350 ml/12 oz. tonic water
squeezed juice of
    1 lemon or lime,
    depending on your
    preference
50 ml/1²/₃ oz. gin

4 ice pop moulds and
4 sticks

MAKES 4

Place a cucumber slice and a lemon slice in each ice pop mould, with room between to fill with the liquid. (If you prefer you can just use cucumber or lemon rather than both, it is up to you.)

Mix the tonic water, lemon or lime juice and gin together in a jug/pitcher and pour into the moulds. Add the sticks in a straight, upright position. Freeze for at least 8 hours or overnight until solid.

When ready to serve, remove the gin and tonic ice pops from their moulds (see page 7) and serve straight away.

STRAWBERRY DAIQUIRI ICE POPS

One of the most popular classic cocktails, daiquiris usually consist of rum, citrus and sugar mixed with a fruit base. These daiquiri pops are strawberry flavour, with a hint of tangy lime.

400 g/14 oz. fresh
   strawberries
40 ml/1¼ oz. spiced rum
20 ml/¾ oz. triple sec
2 tablespoons white
   sugar
squeezed juice of 2 limes
100 ml/3½ oz. clear
   sparkling lemonade

4 ice pop moulds and
4 sticks, blender

MAKES 4

Using a sharp knife, cut the green stalks off the strawberries. Cut 4–5 of the strawberries into slices and place about 5 slices into the bottom of each mould.

Place the remaining strawberries in the blender with the rum, triple sec, sugar lime juice and lemonade and blitz to a smooth purée. Pour the purée into the moulds. Add the sticks in a straight, upright position. Freeze for at least 8 hours or overnight until solid.

When ready to serve, remove the ice pops from their moulds (see page 7) and serve straight away.

POUSSE CAFÉ ICE POPS

I admire the bartenders who in chic Parisian cafés pour multi-layered pousse café cocktail shots with a steady hand to create the perfect rainbow. Getting this effect in an ice pop is much easier, but you need patience as it takes time to freeze the layers. It's worth the wait as they look and taste amazing!

LAYER 1
80 ml/2³/₄ oz. clear sparkling lemonade
15 ml/¹/₂ oz. parfait amour or other violet-coloured liqueur

LAYER 2
80 ml/2³/₄ oz. clear sparkling lemonade
15 ml/¹/₂ oz. blue curaçao

LAYER 3
80 ml/2³/₄ oz. clear sparkling lemonade
10 ml/¹/₂ oz. crème de menthe

LAYER 4
80 ml/2³/₄ oz. pineapple juice
15 ml/¹/₂ oz. coconut rum

LAYER 5
80 ml/2³/₄ oz. clear sparkling lemonade
15 ml/¹/₂ oz. Campari

LAYER 6
80 ml/2³/₄ oz. clear sparkling lemonade
15 ml/¹/₂ oz. grenadine

4 ice pop moulds and 4 sticks

MAKES 4

For each layer, following the numbered order of the ingredients and starting with layer 1, mix together the ingredients and then divide between the moulds and freeze for about 8 hours until solid. Add the sticks in a straight, upright position when you get to the third layer. It is important that each layer is fully frozen before the next layer is added, otherwise the colours will merge and you will not get a perfect rainbow.

When ready to serve, remove the ice pops from their moulds (see page 7) and serve straight away.

CREAM SODA CANDY POPS

These pops are the ultimate in kitsch – cream soda and vodka paired with your favourite fruity candies. It is best to use jelly candies, as some harder sweets will dissolve in frozen liquid. Jelly candies absorb the alcohol and will keep their shape well. If you want to make pretty coloured layers with smaller sweets, then fill each mould a third full with cream soda and add a layer of sweets before freezing and repeating twice more.

80 ml/3 oz. vodka
300 ml/10 oz. cream
   soda
200 g/7 oz. jelly sweets/
   candy such as Fruit
   Pastilles or Haribo

*4 ice pop moulds and
4 sticks*

MAKES 4

Mix together the vodka and cream soda in a jug/pitcher. (Note: it is important not to add any more vodka than stated in this recipe, as it does not freeze well and will mean that your pops may not set.)

Divide the jelly sweets between each of the moulds, balancing them on top of each other but with gaps, so that they nearly fill the moulds. Carefully pour in the vodka mixture, then add the sticks in a straight, upright position. Freeze for at least 8 hours or overnight until solid.

When ready to serve, remove the cream soda candy pops from their moulds (see page 7) and serve straight away.

B52 ICE POPS

A B52 is a layered cocktail shot with flavours of orange, coffee and Irish cream. It translates to these fun, stripy ice pops, which are perfect for parties. Each layer needs time to freeze, so begin these pops a few days before your party. Once the moulds have been removed they will keep in bags in the freezer.

FOR THE ORANGE LAYER
100 ml/3¹/₃ oz. fresh
    orange juice
30 ml/1 oz. orange
    liqueur such as
    Grand Marnier

FOR THE COFFEE LAYER
160 ml/5¹/₂ oz. whole
    milk
30 ml/1 oz. coffee liqueur
    such as Tia Maria

FOR THE IRISH CREAM
LAYER
160 ml/5¹/₂ oz. whole
    milk
40 ml/1¹/₄ oz. Irish cream
    liqueur such as Baileys

4 ice pop moulds and
4 sticks

MAKES 4

Prepare the orange layer first. Whisk together the orange juice and orange liqueur in a jug/pitcher and divide between the moulds, filling them each one-third full. Add the sticks in a straight, upright position. Freeze for at least 8 hours or overnight until solid.

For the second layer, whisk together the milk and coffee liqueur and pour over the frozen orange layer in the moulds to fill two thirds of the way up. Freeze again for a further 8 hours or overnight until solid.

For the Irish cream layer, whisk together the milk and Irish cream liqueur and then pour over the frozen coffee layer. Freeze again for 8 hours or overnight until solid.

When ready to serve, remove the B52 ice pops from their moulds (see page 7) and serve straight away.

TEQUILA SUNRISE POPS

If you are looking for ice pops to serve at a summer party then look no further. Usually, red grenadine is added to the drink which sinks to the bottom to give the sunrise effect. These fun stripy pops are spiked with tequila, with fresh fruity flavours coming from orange and cranberry juices and cherries.

FOR THE ORANGE LAYER
12 glacé or maraschino cocktail cherries
200 ml/6³/4 oz. orange juice
30 ml/1 oz. tequila

FOR THE RED LAYER
100 ml/3¹/3 oz. cranberry juice
20 ml/³/4 oz. grenadine

4 ice pop moulds and 4 sticks

MAKES 4

For the first orange layer, put three cherries into each mould, stacking them slightly so that there is a gap between them that can be filled with the orange juice mixture. Mix together the orange juice and tequila in a jug/pitcher and pour into the moulds to fill them about three-quarters of the way full. Insert the lolly sticks in a straight, upright position. Freeze for 8 hours or overnight until solid.

For the red layer, mix together the cranberry juice and grenadine and then pour into the moulds on top of the frozen orange layer to fill almost to the top. Freeze again for 8 hours or overnight until solid.

When ready to serve, remove the tequila sunrise ice pops from their moulds (see page 7) and serve straight away.

ESPRESSO ICE POPS

These elegant stripy pops have a boozy kick from Tia Maria.
You can substitute other coffee liqueurs but you may need to
reduce the quantity if the alcohol content is higher than 26.5%.
Thinner stripes would look stunning if you have the time.

FOR THE ESPRESSO LAYERS
30 g/2¹/₂ tablespoons
    white sugar
100 ml/3¹/₃ oz. hot
    espresso coffee
40 ml/1¹/₄ oz. Tia Maria
    or other coffee liqueur

FOR THE MILK LAYERS
20 g/1¹/₂ tablespoons
    white sugar
200 ml/6³/₄ oz. whole
    milk

*4 ice pop moulds
and 4 sticks*

MAKES 4

Stir the sugar into the hot coffee until
dissolved and let cool. When cool, mix
together with the Tia Maria in a jug/
pitcher. Pour the coffee mixture into each
mould to fill one-quarter of the way full.
(If you are doing more than four stripes,
add less coffee mixture at this stage,
and in each of the stages below.) Freeze
for at least 8 hours or overnight until solid.
Keep and refrigerate the leftover coffee
mixture until needed again.

For the milk layer, stir the sugar into the
milk until it is completely dissolved. Pour
the milk mixture into the moulds until
they are half-full, keeping the leftover milk
mixture in the fridge until needed again.
Freeze again for around 3 hours. Repeat
the two steps above again so that you
have another layer each of coffee and milk
(or more if doing more layers).

When ready to serve, remove the espresso
ice pops from their moulds (see page 7)
and serve straight away.

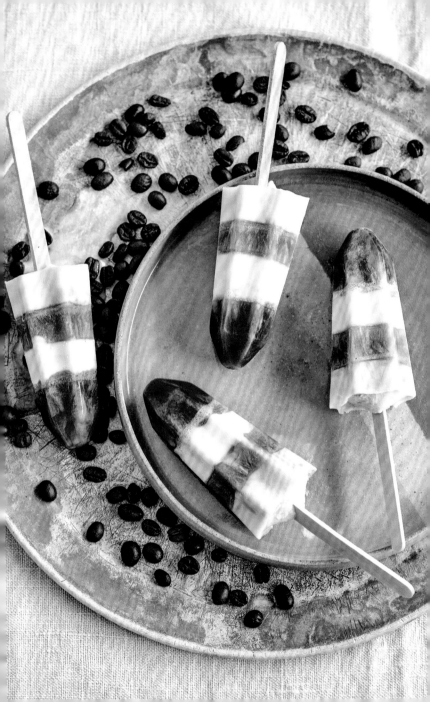

SLUSHIES

BLUEBERRY BUBBLE SLUSHIES

Taiwanese bubble tea, the popular drink, is the inspiration for this slushie. Bubble tea is traditionally made with tapioca pearls, but in this recipe I have used blueberry and lemon flavour bursting juice bubbles (available online from Popaball). They make a vibrant garnish on top of this boozy slushie.

FOR THE BLUEBERRY SYRUP
200 g/7 oz. fresh
   blueberries
60 g/¼ cup white sugar
squeezed juice of
   1 lemon
120 ml/4 oz. water

TO SERVE
12 fresh blueberries
2 long strips of lemon
   zest
20–30 ice cubes
60 ml/2 oz. vodka
2 tablespoons blueberry
   and lemon flavour
   bursting juice bubbles

2 glasses, 2 wooden
skewers

MAKES 2

For the syrup, put the blueberries, sugar and lemon juice in a saucepan with the water and simmer over a gentle heat for about 5–10 minutes until the fruit is soft. Pass the fruit and juice through a sieve/strainer, pressing down with the back of a spoon to release as much juice as possible. Discard any fruit that remains in the strainer. Leave to cool completely.

Just before you are ready to serve, thread the 12 blueberries and lemon zest strips onto the skewers. These will be the garnish for the drinks.

Crush the ice (see page 7). Divide the crushed ice between the two glasses. Add half of the blueberry syrup and half the vodka to each glass and stir to a slushie consistency. Garnish with the bursting bubbles and the fruit skewers. Serve straight away with wide straws to sup the bubbles.

PIÑA COLADA SLUSHIES

Conjuring up scenes of beaches with palm trees overhead, the piña colada is my drink of choice when lying by the pool. Sadly, this is not always possible – but serving this slushie at home will hopefully transport your mind to sunnier climes. For a totally tropical feel, use hollowed out coconuts or pineapples as cups. If you want to make the slushie boozier, add a little more rum with the extra pineapple juice.

125 ml/4 oz. coconut milk
125 ml/4 oz. coconut rum
such as Malibu
60 ml/2 oz. vodka
375 ml/13 oz. pineapple
juice

TO SERVE
200 ml/6³/4 oz.
pineapple juice (you
might not need all
of this)
maraschino cocktail
cherries and pineapple
wedges on a cocktail
stick/toothpick, to
garnish

*freezerproof lidded
container, 2 glasses or
hollowed out pineapple
or coconut shells*

SERVES 2

Mix the coconut milk well to get rid of any large clumps that sometimes form at the top of the can. In the freezerproof container, whisk together the coconut milk, rum, vodka, and pineapple juice until well blended. Cover the container with the lid and freeze overnight.

When you are ready to serve, remove the container from the freezer. Do not worry if the mixture has separated, this is normal. Using a fork, crush the mixture to small ice crystals. It should only be semi-frozen due to the vodka and easy to crush. Add the extra pineapple juice slowly and mix to make a slushie consistency – you might not need all of the juice depending on the size of your glass.

Divide the slushie between the glasses or pineapple/coconut shells. Add straws and serve straight away, topped with the cherry and wedges of pineapple on a stick.

BLOODY MARY SLUSHIES

This super-refreshing version of a bloody mary will become your 'morning-after' drink of choice! A spicy tomato slushed ice is served over vodka. Of course, many people have personal preferences over the ingredients used to season their bloody mary, so make up the tomato ice to your taste, whether you add more or less Tabasco, lemon juice or even horseradish.

250 ml/8$^{1}/_{2}$ oz. tomato
   juice
dash of Tabasco sauce
2 teaspoons
   Worcestershire sauce
celery salt and cracked
   black pepper

TO SERVE
120 ml/4 oz. vodka
celery sticks, to garnish

large 14-hole ice cube
tray, blender, 2 martini
glasses

SERVES 2

In a jug/pitcher, whisk together the tomato juice, Tabasco and Worcestershire sauce. Season to taste with celery salt and cracked black pepper – add a little more than usual as freezing diminishes the flavour slightly. Pour the tomato juice mixture into the large ice cube tray and freeze until solid, preferably overnight. Of course, you can prepare the ice cubes well in advance and keep them in the freezer until you require them.

When you are ready to serve, crush the bloody mary ice cubes (see page 7), ideally in a suitable blender or snow cone machine. Pour half of the vodka into each of the glasses and top each with half of the crushed tomato ice. Garnish with celery sticks and serve straight away.

U-BOAT SLUSHIES

Named after the German name for a submarine, a u-boat cocktail consists of a shot glass of vodka submerged inside a glass of beer. The combination of beer and vodka is a match made in heaven when it comes to creating a frozen slushie, as the vodka prevents the beer from freezing solidly, leaving you with the undiluted beer flavour. To serve, add a little more beer or lemonade depending on how strong you want it to be.

275 ml/9^1/$_2$ oz. lager
  or light beer
200 ml/6^3/$_4$ oz. clear
  sparkling lemonade
  (use sugar-free if you
  don't want it too
  sweet)
50 ml/1^2/$_3$ oz. vodka

TO SERVE

400 ml/14 oz. clear
  sparkling lemonade
  or lager/light beer
lime wedges, to garnish
  (optional)

*freezerproof lidded
container, 2 beer glasses*

SERVES 2

Mix together the lager, lemonade and vodka in a jug/pitcher. Pour into the freezerproof container, cover with the lid and freeze overnight.

When ready to serve, use a fork to crush the mixture to create a slushie texture. Due to the alcohol content it should only be semi-frozen and easy to crush.

Divide the slushie between the two glasses and add half of the beer or lemonade, as preferred, to each glass. Garnish with lime wedges, if desired, and serve straight away.

SANGRIA SLUSHIES

With its bold red wine, brandy and orange flavours, a cold glass
of sangria is so evocative of warm, sunny Spanish holidays!
Because slushies contain a lot of ice they can be quite watery,
so the homemade full-flavoured red wine syrup in this drink
ensures a punchy taste. You don't need to stick to oranges, feel
free to add extra fruits of your choice to serve.

FOR THE RED WINE SYRUP
400 ml/14 oz. full-bodied
    red wine
200 ml/6³/₄ oz. orange
    juice
100 g/scant ¹/₂ cup white
    sugar

TO SERVE
about 40 ice cubes
thinly sliced oranges
    or clementines
120 ml/4 oz. brandy

2 glasses

SERVES 2

In a saucepan, combine the red wine,
orange juice and sugar. Simmer over
a medium heat, stirring to dissolve the
sugar, until the liquid has reduced by half
and looks syrupy. Remove from the heat
and leave to cool completely, then chill
in the refrigerator until needed.

When you are ready to serve, crush the
ice (see page 7) and divide between two
glasses. Add a couple of orange or
clementine slices to each. Add half the red
wine syrup and half the brandy to each
glass. Give the drinks a stir and then serve
straight away, with straws and additional
orange slices to garnish, if you like.

FIRECRACKER SLUSHIES

The famous American firecracker ice pops are very patriotic with their red, white and blue stripes, flavoured with cherry, lemonade and blue raspberry. Why not try this delicious and vibrant homemade slushie version?

FOR THE BLUE RASPBERRY SLUSHIES
30 ml/1 oz. blue curaçao
100 ml/3⅓ oz. vodka
30 ml/1 oz. Chambord or other raspberry liqueur
100 ml/3⅓ oz. clear sparkling lemonade

FOR THE LEMONADE SLUSHIES
125 ml/4 oz. vodka
180 ml/6 oz. clear sparkling lemonade
squeezed juice of 1 lemon

FOR THE CHERRY SLUSHIES
125 ml/4 oz. vodka
180 ml/6 oz. cherry juice

TO SERVE
3 fresh strawberries

3 freezerproof lidded containers, 3 tall glasses

MAKES 3

Mix together the liquids for each of the three slushie flavours and place them in separate freezerproof boxes. Cover with the lids and freeze overnight.

When you are ready to serve, use a fork to crush the ice mixtures to create a slushie texture.

Layer up the three slushies in each glass, starting with the blue, then the white, then the red. Garnish each glass with a sliced strawberry and serve straight away with straws for slurping and stirring.

SEA BREEZE SLUSHIES

This sea breeze slushie has a really tangy flavour from the grapefruit and cranberry. Like all of these recipes, it can be prepared ahead and so is great for parties. If you want to create a two-tone mixed slushie, make one batch of the recipe below with just grapefruit juice and one with just cranberry – using 185 ml/6$\frac{1}{4}$ oz. of juice to each 125 ml/4 oz. of vodka.

125 ml/4 oz. vodka
125 ml/4 oz. cranberry
　　juice
60 ml/2 oz. grapefruit
　　juice

TO SERVE
200 ml/6$\frac{3}{4}$ oz.
　　cranberry juice
2 tablespoons grenadine
60 ml/2 oz. vodka

*freezerproof lidded
container, 2 glasses*

SERVES 2

Mix together the vodka, cranberry juice and grapefruit juice in the freezerproof container. Cover with the lid and freeze overnight.

When you are ready to serve, remove the vodka mixture from the freezer and crush with a fork to make a slushie consistency. Pour half of the cranberry juice into each glass and add half the grenadine and vodka to each. Place a large spoonful of the ice slushie in the middle of each glass and serve straight away, with straws and a cocktail umbrella or stirrer, if you like.

MOSCOW MULE SLUSHIES

As a child I was a big fan of ginger beer, perhaps because it was novelist Enid Blyton's choice of tipple for her characters 'The Famous Five' in some of my favourite books. The Moscow mule cocktail seemed a natural progression for me as I grew up – what is not to like about ginger, lime and vodka! The air in the kitchen can become eye-wateringly spicy if you use a fiery ginger beer to make up this syrup – you have been warned!

FOR THE GINGER BEER SYRUP
600 ml/20 oz. sparkling
    ginger beer
50 g/3½ tablespoons
    white sugar

TO SERVE
120 ml/4 oz. vodka
4 fresh limes
about 40 ice cubes

blender, 2 glasses

MAKES 2

Combine the ginger beer and sugar in a saucepan. Simmer over a gentle heat, stirring to dissolve the sugar, until the liquid has reduced by about half and looks syrupy. Remove from the heat and leave to cool completely. Chill in the refrigerator until you are ready to use.

When you are ready to serve, peel long strips of lime zest from one of the limes ready for the garnish. Squeeze the juice from all 4 limes and reserve. Add the ginger beer syrup, vodka, lime juice and ice to a blender and blitz for a few seconds until the ice has crushed and you have a slushie texture. Pour into the glasses, top with the reserved zest and serve straight away with straws.

MINT JULEP SLUSHIES

The mint julep is my favourite tipple at the popular horserace the Kentucky Derby. Every year, they create a spruced version with additions such as elderflower and Earl Grey tea. Here, I've turned the classic cocktail into a slushie, with a mint syrup and bourbon served over crushed ice. It makes a delicious treat for any whisky lover. Juleps are traditionally served in tankards which look nice for a special occasion.

FOR THE MINT SYRUP
160 ml/5¹/₂ oz. water
100 g/scant ¹/₂ cup white
    sugar
6 sprigs of fresh mint

TO SERVE
about 20–30 ice cubes
about 60–80 ml/
    2–2³/₄ oz. bourbon
extra fresh mint sprigs,
    to garnish

*blender for crushing ice,
2 glasses or tankards*

MAKES 2

Place the water in a saucepan with the sugar and mint and bring to the boil. Turn down the heat and simmer for about 5 minutes, swirling the pan a little, until you have a thin syrup. Remove from the heat and leave to cool completely. Chill in the refrigerator until you are ready to use.

When you are ready to serve, crush the ice (see page 7) and divide between two glasses. Pour half of the mint syrup and half of the bourbon into each glass. Stir and then serve straight away with straws and garnished with extra sprigs of mint.

INDEX